Jr. Social Studies Investigator

By Stacie Hutton

Pieces of Learning

© 2005 Pieces of Learning
CLC0351
ISBN   1-931334-64-1
Graphic Production by Sharolyn Hill
Art by Denise Tadlock
www.piecesoflearning.com

Cover: Students Jordan Steele and Matt Chenoweth
Cover Photo by Mark Chenoweth   Cover Art by John Steele

Table of Contents

Directions for Teachers/Adult Leaders

The Goal of this book is to provide an introduction to and preliminary practice in using primary source documents. It includes . . .

- activities to engage convergent learners through investigative activities.

- activities to engage divergent learners through creating clues and setting up their own historical scenes.

- guidance in preliminary use of the inquiry method of instruction.

- guidance in preliminary use of primary source documents.

- guidance in using logical reasoning to solve the scene.

- activities that involve sequencing and cause/effect relationships necessary for many state and national social studies exams.

- guidance in gaining a better understanding of the past.

Students will be able to . . .

- practice necessary social studies skills using time lines, identifying cause and effect relationships, and sequencing of events.

- through structured inquiry, investigate various historical topics.

- acquire and practice the techniques utilized in formal historical research.

- apply logical reasoning skills to solve scenes.

- discuss the significance of each historical topic.

- view history as an interesting field of study, a "mystery" rather than a subject of memorization.

About The Clues

- Most clues are contained in each chapter; others are everyday items.

- If you have difficulty finding a certain item, make the clue or locate a substitute item.

- Many clues "mimic" as primary sources. Most have been fictionalized. Some clues are historical recreations. However, each clue is based upon historical documents.

- Yard sales and thrift stores may offer affordable items to be used as clues.

- Each clue has an explanation for its use in the scene.

- If you do the "follow-up" activity of creating another clue, encourage students to think about what clues they believe were missing or should have been in the scene based upon their research about the historical topic/subject.

- For effect photocopy 17th and 18th century clues on parchment-type paper.

Implementing the Activities in Your Classroom

Whole class – Students move from research to investigating the scene in small groups.

Small groups – If your group is small enough, create an "investigative team" and allow them to present results of their investigation together.

Procedure

1. Set up clues/props for each scene. Become part of the process – add *your* own clues.

2. Prior to students investigating the scene, have students read through all preliminary materials.

3. Have students investigate the scene and complete the investigation sheet.

4. Have students research the scene.

During this time, guide students or allow them to work independently. The *"Think About It"* page guides students while they investigate. You may choose whether or not to allow students to use this sheet.

You may choose to do follow-up activities and/or discussion questions.

Other Recommendations

Have students practice inferencing skills prior to initiating the activities.

Review all preliminary activities with students (*Letter From "Butch," What is History, All About the Clues, How to Investigate Historical Clues,*) before beginning the historical chapters containing scenes for students to solve.

Although the historical background section is intended for your use, you may choose to allow students to use it instead of research materials. However, the intent is for students to utilize various research methods and primary sources. Encyclopedias are particularly recommended.

Use this book to build research skills and to gain meaning from non-fiction selections.

Use a magnifying glass with clues in the scene to simulate "investigator."

Chapter 1

Preliminary Activities

? ? ? ? ? ? ? ? ? ? ? ?

History is a Mystery

Dear History Investigators,

My name is Captain Butch, and like other cats I have nine lives. During those nine lives I have witnessed many exciting events from history. I have also met some important people along the way.

While many cats hunt mice and live a quiet life, my colleagues and I have hunted historical clues. These clues will help you to understand the past very well.

If you have a cat or have observed a cat, you may notice that the cat knows a lot about the past. Maybe it knows when you have to get up for school in the morning, or it knows exactly when you have to do your homework at night. Cats learn these things by watching things repeat themselves. You probably have noticed your cat quietly lying in a corner watching your every move. That is why cats are good investigators. Cats listen and observe.

Throughout this book you will see things that I have collected throughout my nine lives. Wait 'til you "see what the cats have dragged in."

Butch

What is History? How Do We Unlock Clues from the Past?

Every moment in time that has passed us is a moment of history . . .

- What you learned in school yesterday
- What you had for lunch yesterday

These things are *your* "history." Like footprints in the sand, each day you are leaving behind a piece of your own history.

Why is it important to remember the past? What if you did not remember what you learned in school yesterday? It might hurt you on a test or quiz tomorrow.

What if you did not remember what you ate for lunch? Perhaps you did not like it. If you do not remember, maybe you will eat it again and repeat the mistake!

If you are not be able to recall what you learned or had for lunch yesterday, what things could you do to help yourself remember?

If you have trouble remembering what happened yesterday, imagine trying to remember things that happened <u>years</u> ago. This is the problem faced by people who study history, or **historians**. They use journals, diaries, photographs, and records to help them unlock clues from the past.

Other things, too, can be an important historical document – newspaper articles and the papers of important people like Presidents are examples. Some clues like feather pens help us identify the time period.

All About Clues

What is a clue? A clue gives information that can help you solve something. Just like a puzzle piece, it is part of the solution to a puzzle.

Think about your grandparents or your parents. What clues could you discover to see what they were like when they were your age?

What would their report cards tell you?

What would pictures/photographs tell you?

What other clues would help you learn about their past?

Of course, we will not be able to find out everything about them or other people/events that happened in the past because we weren't there. This is why history is the biggest mystery of them all.

We can solve the mystery of history by looking at the clues left behind by those who lived it.

Historical Clues are often the important papers left behind by those who lived a historical event.

Which of these clues do you think would give the best information about a historical **person/event**?

- Diary entries
- Important records
- Photographs/pictures
- Newspaper articles

All of the above items help us solve the mystery of history.

A diary or journal is a **historical clue** because it has a date and often provides an understanding of the time in history. Other clues, like candles or feather pens, help us identify the historical **time period**.

How to Investigate Historical Clues

The three things to look for on historical papers are **names, dates,** and **locations**. Some papers may also have a **title**. These items can help you begin researching to discover the history behind the clue.

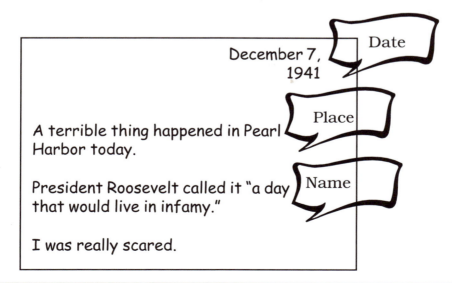

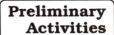

What kind of historical paper is the example on page 10?
Diary entry?
Newspaper article?
Paper written by an important person like a President?

How do you know that this was not written by an important historical person like a President?

When you are investigating history, it is important to **ask questions**. First, you may begin with a big question; then after investigating you may have smaller questions that, if you answer them, may help you answer the big question.

For instance, imagine that you came home from school and your room was a mess. Just like history, you were not there when it happened so it is a mystery to you. What might be a big question you would ask?

_____

_____

Now, suppose after investigating your room you find a bracelet that does not belong to you. What would be your smaller question?

_____

_____

_____

Now it is your turn to make a **clue**. In the space below, write an imaginary diary entry of a person who had lived through a major weather event – snowstorm, rainstorm, earthquake, tornado, etc. Do not name the event. Share your entry with classmates to see if they can discover the event.

_____

_____

_____

_____

_____

Remember, most questions whether big or small begin with: **who, what, when, where, why,** and **how.**

When you investigate historical clues in these units, they will be in a **scene**. Think of how a detective investigates a crime scene. The detective investigates **clues** at the scene of the crime.

While you investigate, you will be using the
<u>Historical Method of Investigation</u>.

The steps are:

1. What is the big question?

2. Mark the approximate time period on the time line.

3. Develop a hypothesis to answer the big question.

4. List the clues you see in the scene. List important items about each clue.

5. What is your **hypothesis** about what is going on in the scene?

6. What do you need to know about each clue? List your smaller questions to help you answer the bigger questions.

7. Research your final answer to the big questions. Use the ***"Think About It"*** page to help you. Hint: The answers to your smaller questions will help you answer the bigger questions.

8. Was your hypothesis correct?

9. What else do you want to know? List other questions you have about this historical topic.

Chapter 2

Presidents

Biography of George Washington

America's first President and commander of the Continental Army during the American Revolution, George Washington was one of our nation's beloved leaders.

Born in Westmoreland County, Virginia, on February 22, 1732, Washington was educated in mathematics, reading the classics, and surveying. Washington remained at his family's estate until his father's death in 1743. Washington then went to live with his brother Lawrence at his estate at Mount Vernon.

Washington's education continued in surveying; however, Washington's training would soon involve the military. He learned quickly and eventually became commander of the Continental Army that would defeat the British and gain independence.

After America gained its independence, Washington participated in another important event as a delegate from Virginia. Washington traveled to Philadelphia in 1787, to draft the United States Constitution.

Once this document was in place, Washington, highly admired, was unanimously elected the first President of The United States. He took office in New York on April 30, 1789. He remained in office until 1797.

He died at his Mount Vernon estate on December 14, 1799.

Washington Scene

Goal of Scene

To recognize the accomplishments of George Washington

Description of Scene

The scene takes place in George Washington's home just before he would travel to New York City in 1789, to be inaugurated as the first president of the United States.

Clues and Other Items in Scene

Included Clues
  • See page 18
Optional Clues
  • Desk
  • Feather Pen
  • Ink Bottle

Setting up the Scene

Place all items on a desk or another hard surface.

<u>Higher Level Thinking Activities</u>
Discussion / research questions

  • Why was Washington so admired?
  • Why was Washington in New York?
  • What were the effects of Washington leading America in winning the Revolutionary War? Name an effect on the nation and on George Washington's life.

<u>Follow-up Activities</u>

  • Have students decide which of Washington's accomplishments was the most important:
    • Winning the Revolution
    • Becoming President
    • Signing the U.S. Constitution

  • Have students create a clue that may have appeared in this scene. (see page 10 for help)

  • Have students imagine what they might say if they were the first president of the United States. Students should consider things that would be important to tell the citizens of the new country.

Investigating The Scene

1. Your big questions:
   a. To whom do these clues belong?

   b. Why are they important?

2. Mark approximate time period on the time line below.

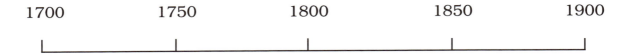

3. List the clues you see in the scene. List important items about each clue (see page 10 *"How to Investigate Historical Clues"* for help).

4. What is your hypothesis about what is going on in the scene?

5. What do you need to know about each clue? List your smaller questions to help you answer the bigger questions.

6. Research your final answer to the big questions. Use the *"Think About It"* page to help you. Hint: The answers to your smaller questions will help you answer the bigger questions.

7. Was your hypothesis correct?

8. What else do you want to know? List other questions you have about this historical topic.

Think About It

It could be ...

Circle One:

- Thomas Jefferson

- Abraham Lincoln

- George Washington

... because ...

Mark the box matching the reasons **WHY**.

❑ The person was a President

❑ The person lived during the dates listed on the clue

❑ The person was in the military

❑ The person wrote the Declaration of Independence

❑ The person wrote the Emancipation Proclamation

It could NOT be ...

Circle Two:

- Thomas Jefferson

- Abraham Lincoln

- George Washington

... because ...

Mark the box matching the reasons **WHY NOT**.

❑ The person <u>was not</u> an inventor/architect

❑ The person <u>did not</u> live during this time

❑ The person <u>was not</u> in the military

❑ The person <u>did not</u> write the Declaration of Independence

❑ The person <u>did not</u> write the Emancipation Proclamation

Provided Clues – George Washington

Commander
of the
Continental
Army

--- Cut Here ---

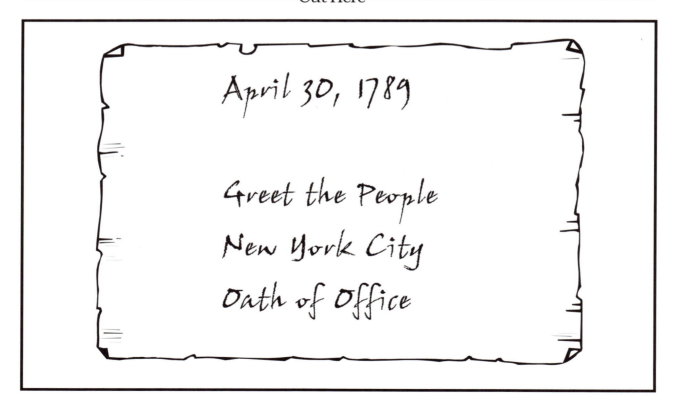

April 30, 1789

Greet the People

New York City

Oath of Office

Biography of Thomas Jefferson

Thomas Jefferson, the President of the United States and author of the Declaration of Independence, was born April 13, 1743, in Virginia. When Jefferson was fourteen years old, his father died leaving the entire estate to Jefferson.

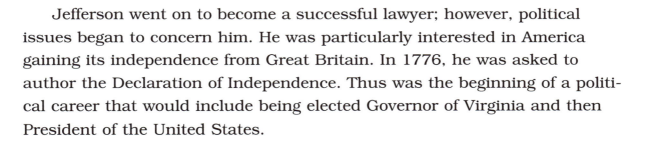

He lived on a large estate in Virginia with six sisters and one brother. After the family tragedy, Jefferson entered the school of James Marry near Charlottesville, Virginia. He then attended the college of William and Mary in Virginia. Upon completing college in 1762, Jefferson studied law.

Jefferson went on to become a successful lawyer; however, political issues began to concern him. He was particularly interested in America gaining its independence from Great Britain. In 1776, he was asked to author the Declaration of Independence. Thus was the beginning of a political career that would include being elected Governor of Virginia and then President of the United States.

Beyond his political career, Thomas Jefferson was an architect and inventor. He designed his own home, Monticello, and his home included many of his inventions.

Jefferson died July 4, 1826, fifty years after the signing of the Declaration of Independence.

Thomas Jefferson

Goal of Scene
To recognize the accomplishments of Thomas Jefferson

Description of Scene
The scene takes place at Jefferson's Monticello home. The year in which the scene takes place is not particularly important. The scene showcases the accomplishments of Thomas Jefferson.

Clues and Other Items in Scene
Included Clues
  • See page 23
Optional Clues
  • Desk
  • Feather Pen
  • Ink Bottle

Setting up the Scene
Place all items on a desk or another hard surface.

<u>Higher Level Thinking Activities</u>
Discussion / research questions

- How do you know Thomas Jefferson was a man of many talents?
- What would America be like had Jefferson not been the author of the Declaration of Independence?
- What does it tell you about Jefferson that he authored the Declaration of Independence and designed his own home?
- What were the effects of the Declaration of Independence?

<u>Follow-up Activities</u>

- Create a clue that may have appeared in this scene. (see page 10 for help)

- In the spirit of Jefferson, have students design an illustration of their dream home complete with secret passages and inventions.

- Have students re-write the Declaration of Independence substituting the King or "He" and other words for something or someone who desires independence.

Investigating The Scene

1. Your big questions:
   a. To whom do these clues belong?

   b. Why are they important?

2. Mark approximate time period on the time line below.

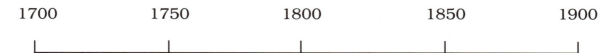

   1700   1750   1800   1850   1900

3. List the clues you see in the scene. List important items about each clue (see page 10 *"How to Investigate Historical Clues"* for help).

4. What is your hypothesis about what is going on in the scene?

5. What do you need to know about each clue? List your smaller questions to help you answer the bigger questions.

6. Research your final answer to the big questions. Use the *"Think About It"* page to help you. Hint: The answers to your smaller questions will help you answer the bigger questions.

7. Was your hypothesis correct?

8. What else do you want to know? List other questions you have about this historical topic.

Think About It

It could be ...

Circle One:

- Thomas Jefferson

- Abraham Lincoln

- George Washington

... because ...

Mark the box matching the reasons
WHY.

❑ The person was a President

❑ The person lived during the
dates listed on the clue

❑ The person was in the military

❑ The person wrote the
Declaration of Independence

❑ The person wrote the Emancipation Proclamation

It could NOT be ...

Circle Two:

- Thomas Jefferson

- Abraham Lincoln

- George Washington

... because ...

Mark the box matching the reasons
WHY NOT.

❑ The person <u>was not</u> an inventor/
architect

❑ The person <u>did not</u> live during
this time

❑ The person <u>was not</u> in the
military

❑ The person <u>did not</u> write the
Declaration of Independence

❑ The person <u>did not</u> write the
Emancipation Proclamation

Provided Clues – Thomas Jefferson

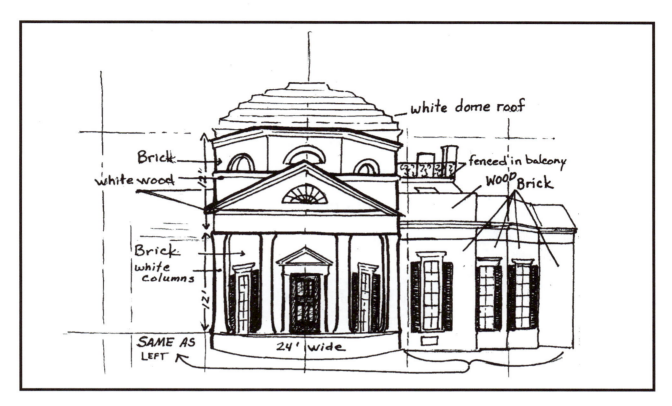

-- Cut Here --

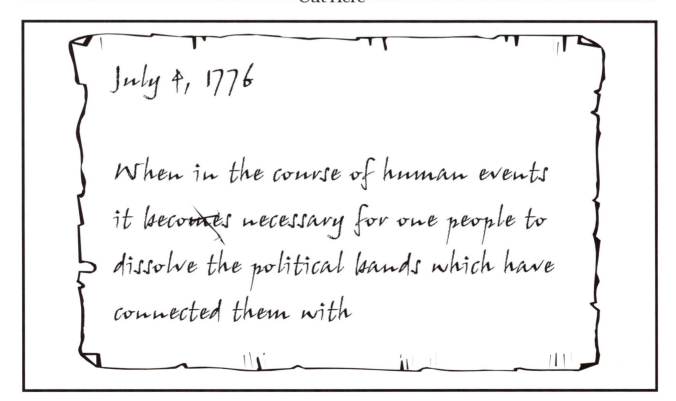

Biography of Abraham Lincoln

President Abraham Lincoln was born on February 12, 1809, in a log cabin in the backwoods of Kentucky. Life in those times was hard; young Abe would spend many hours helping his family tame the frontier land. Because of those hardships, a young Abe was able to attend what would total one year of school.

Despite poverty and lack of education, Abe Lincoln was determined to rise above his disadvantages. An avid reader, he taught himself the law. Lincoln became such a well-known lawyer that it lead to a career in politics. Lincoln was elected as an Illinois State Representative and then in 1861 as President of the United States.

When Abraham Lincoln was President, the people of the United States were divided on the issue of slavery, and America went to war to decide the issue. President Lincoln was against slavery and wrote the Emancipation Proclamation to help end slavery. Sadly, President Lincoln was killed by an assassin shortly after the Civil War ended.

Abraham Lincoln

Goal of Scene
To recognize the accomplishments of Abraham Lincoln

Description of Scene
The scene takes place at Lincoln's White House office in 1863, just before Lincoln is scheduled to travel to Gettysburg, Pennsylvania, to deliver the famous Gettysburg address. The Emancipation Proclamation notes also appear in the scene to show what else Lincoln was working on in the year 1863.

Clues and Other Items in Scene
Included Clues
- See page 28

Optional Clues
- Desk
- Feather Pen
- Ink Bottle

Setting up the Scene
Place all items on a desk or another hard surface.

<u>Higher Level Thinking Activities</u>
Discussion/ research questions
- Why was it important for President Abraham Lincoln to go to Gettysburg?
- What were some of the problems Lincoln faced during his Presidency? How did he solve them?

<u>Follow-up Activities</u>

- Why was the Emancipation Proclamation so important? Explain in 3 or 4 sentences.

- Create a clue that may have appeared in this scene. (see page 10 for help)

- Have students write and prepare an important statement after a tragedy. Like Lincoln, encourage students to select their words carefully.

- Have students circle important words in the Emancipation Proclamation, and replace them with other words. Have them write a paragraph or respond orally as to how the new words affect the meaning of the document.

Investigating The Scene

1. Your big questions:
   a. To whom do these clues belong?

   b. Why are they important?

2. Mark approximate time period on the time line below.

1700	1750	1800	1850	1900

3. List the clues you see in the scene. List important items about each clue (see page 10 *"How to Investigate Historical Clues"* for help).

4. What is your hypothesis about what is going on in the scene?

5. What do you need to know about each clue? List your smaller questions to help you answer the bigger questions.

6. Research your final answer to the big questions. Use the *"Think About It"* page to help you. Hint: The answers to your smaller questions will help you answer the bigger questions.

7. Was your hypothesis correct?

8. What else do you want to know? List other questions you have about this historical topic.

Think About It

It could be ...

Circle One:

- Thomas Jefferson

- Abraham Lincoln

- George Washington

... because ...

Mark the box matching the reasons **WHY**.

❑ The person was a President

❑ The person lived during the dates listed on the clue

❑ The person was in the military

❑ The person wrote the Declaration of Independence

❑ The person wrote the Emancipation Proclamation

It could NOT be ...

Circle Two:

- Thomas Jefferson

- Abraham Lincoln

- George Washington

... because ...

Mark the box matching the reasons **WHY NOT**.

❑ The person <u>was not</u> an inventor/ architect

❑ The person <u>did not</u> live during this time

❑ The person <u>was not</u> in the military

❑ The person <u>did not</u> write the Declaration of Independence

❑ The person <u>did not</u> write the Emancipation Proclamation

Provided Clues – Abraham Lincoln

Appointments

November 19, 1863

Gettysburg, Pennsylvania

speech – dedication of the

national cemetery

-- Cut Here --

On this 1st day of January, AD 1863

order and declare that all persons

held as slaves within said

designated states and parts of states

are henceforward shall be free

End of Chapter Activities

1. Have students compare/contrast the accomplishments of Lincoln, Washington, and Jefferson. Show likeness and differences through a chart or Venn diagram.

2. Have students select among Lincoln, Washington, and Jefferson and make a scrapbook showcasing his life.

3. Write a letter to the three Presidents about life in America today. Students should determine what this person might consider important.

4. Have the students debate which of the three presidents made the most lasting impact upon America.

Chapter 3

Famous Inventors

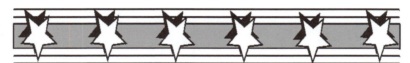

Historical Background
Thomas Edison

Perhaps one of the greatest inventors in American history, Thomas Edison held 1,093 patents – the most ever held by a single person. His contributions include inventing the electrical light and the phonograph to making improvements upon others.

Born on February 11, 1847, Edison was the youngest of seven children. As a child, Edison asked many questions. His mother, a teacher, essentially home-schooled him. Perhaps the most eventful moment of his childhood came when at the age of fifteen Edison rescued the son of a telegraph operator from being struck by a railroad car. Although he had hearing difficulties prior to this, the accident perhaps magnified the condition. For his bravery, Edison was awarded with telegraph lessons from the operator. He became so proficient that he extended himself by making improvements to the existing telegraph.

Edison's interest in improving the telegraph would lead to the construction of a research laboratory in Menlo Park, New Jersey – the most advanced laboratory of its time.

There, Edison and assistants began research on a variety of inventions including the electric light. In 1878, Edison began to research the electric light and decided upon developing an incandescent light for household use. After experimenting with various filaments, they finally used sewing thread burned by carbon.

The experiment proved successful. During the next several years, Edison worked to make the invention more practical by encouraging the construction of power plants.

Edison died in 1931.

Thomas Edison Scene

Goal

- Recognize the accomplishments of Thomas Edison
- Appreciate how this inventor changed the world

Description of Scene

This scene takes place in 1879, at Edison's lab in Menlo Park, New Jersey, just as Edison is testing many filaments to make electricity flow through to produce light. Finally, burned sewing thread would work. Edison's dream would also include making electricity available in all American homes so that the electric light would be more practical.

Clues

- Sewing thread
- Pencil carbon shavings
- Thin wire
- Notes on invention (page 34)
- Table

For effect, you may have assorted scientific equipment in the scene.

Setting up the scene

Reserve an approximate 10' x 8' area of your classroom. Place all items on a table or another hard surface.

Higher Level Thinking Activities
Discussion Questions

- Why was Edison concerned about electricity in American homes?

- What does the fact that Edison tried many filaments tell you about inventing?

- Think of an invention today that not many people own. How could more people own this invention?

Follow-up Activities

- Have students list the items we now have because of this invention.

- Have students imagine a world in which the electric light did not exist.

- Have students create an advertisement promoting this invention.

- Have students brainstorm a list of invention ideas that are impractical at this time and what would need to happen to make them practical.

- Have students create another clue that may have appeared in this scene.

Investigating the Scene

1. Your big question:
   Whose lab/workshop are you in?

2. Mark approximate time period on the time line below.

   1800   1850   1900   1950   2000

3. List the clues you see in the scene. List important items about each clue (see page 10 *"How to Investigate Historical Clues"* for help).

4. What is your hypothesis about what is going on in the scene?

5. What do you need to know about each clue? List your smaller questions to help you answer the big question.

6. Research your final answer to the big question. Use *"Think About It"* to help you. Hint: The answers to your smaller questions will help you answer the big question.

7. Was your hypothesis correct?

8. What else do you want to know? List other questions you have about this historical topic.

- -

Think About It

This invention changed the world in all the ways except:

   A. People could do work at night
   B. People would not need candles
   C. Reduced the need for kerosene lamps
   D. Businesses could not stay open as long

What is another effect this invention has had upon the world? The effect could be either positive or negative.

_____

_____

Provided Clues – Thomas Edison

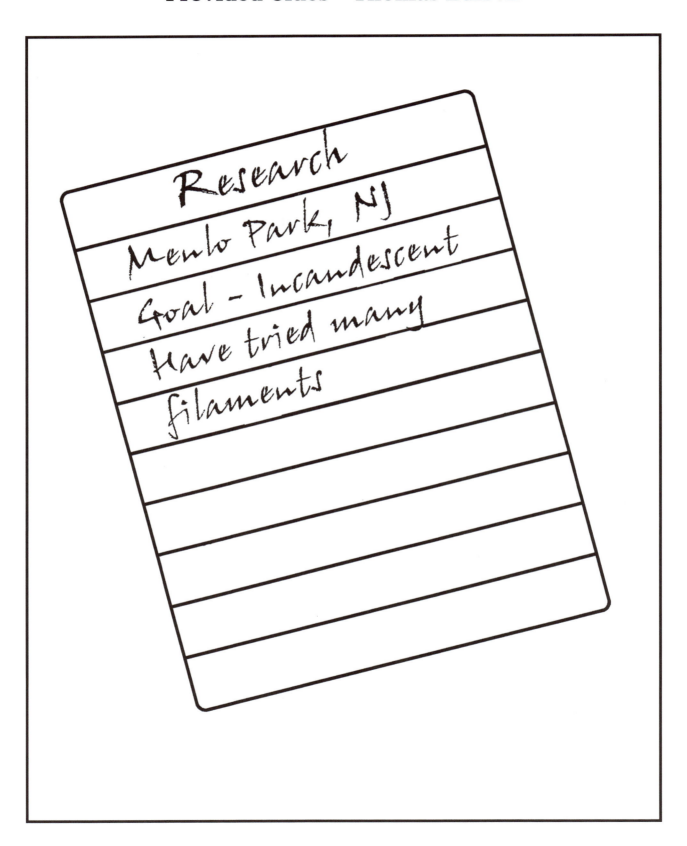

Research
Menlo Park, NJ
Goal – Incandescent
Have tried many
filaments

Historical Background – Henry Ford

Founder of the Ford Motor Company, Henry Ford revolutionized the automotive industry with his invention of the assembly line.

Born in 1863, on a farm in Michigan, Ford was immersed at a young age on the parts of machines, particularly those on the farm. By the age of 16, he became a machinist and later an engineer.

As a young engineer, Ford became interested in the automobile. The invention was relatively new at this time. Ford built a gasoline engine in 1893, and an automobile in 1896. This success allowed him to establish the Ford Motor Company in 1903.

Like most automobile makers of the time, Ford manufactured only expensive automobiles. Thus, only the wealthy could afford one.

Ford decided that he wanted to make automobiles affordable to those less wealthy. Ford, along with his employees, developed an assembly line method that moved parts among the workers. Once the part reached the worker, he/she would complete a task. The results of this method were a success. The assembly time of a Ford reduced from 12 ½ man-hours to 1 ½ man-hours. Thus, the price of a Model T Ford originally $825 was $290 in 1924. More people could now afford a car.

Ford died in 1947.

Henry Ford Scene

Goal
- Recognize the accomplishments of Henry Ford
- Appreciate how this inventor changed the world

Description of Scene
This scene takes place around 1909 in Ford's office about the time Ford decided to manufacture only the Model T Ford to make it less expensive to customers. His assembly line plan using a conveyor belt significantly reduced the amount of time needed to produce a Model T. Thus, the Model T became more affordable to the average American.

Clues
- Plans/notes on assembly line (page 38)
- Plans for Model T (page 38)

Setting Up the Scene
Reserve an approximate 10' x 8' area of your classroom. Place all items on a table or another hard surface.

<u>Higher Level Activities</u>
Discussion Questions
- Why did Ford's assembly line make automobiles less expensive?

- Do you think there are any advantages to just one person building an item?

<u>Follow-up Activities</u>
- Have students imagine if Henry Ford had not decided to try to make cars less expensive. How would the world be different?

- Have students create an advertisement promoting this invention.

- Have students test making a paper airplane by themselves for a period of 10 minutes and then conduct an assembly line approach in a group of four for a period of ten minutes. Have students record results and discuss.

- Have students brainstorm how they think the assembly line may be replaced or improved in the future.

- Have students create another clue that may have appeared in this scene.

Investigating the Scene

1. Your big question:
   Whose lab/workshop are you in?

2. Mark approximate time period on the time line below.

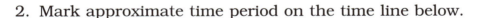

| 1800 | 1850 | 1900 | 1950 | 2000 |

3. List the clues you see in the scene. List important items about each clue (see page 10 ***"How to Investigate Historical Clues"*** for help).

4. What is your hypothesis about what is going on in the scene?

5. What do you need to know about each clue? List your smaller questions to help you answer the big question.

6. Research your final answer to the big question. Use ***"Think About It"*** to help you. Hint: The answers to your smaller questions will help you answer the big question.

7. Was your hypothesis correct?

8. What else do you want to know? List other questions you have about this historical topic.

- -

Think About It

This invention changed the world in all the ways except:

   A. Made cars faster to make
   B. Automobiles became less expensive
   C. Reduced horse and buggy travel
   D. Reduced the need for metal, steel

What is another effect this invention has had upon the world? The effect could be either positive or negative.

_____

_____

Provided Clues – Henry Ford

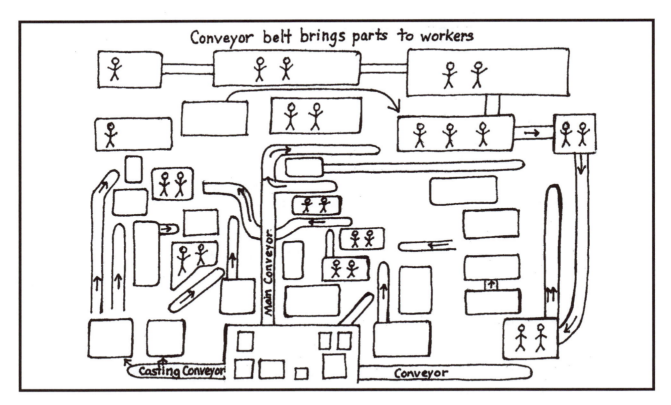

Conveyor belt brings parts to workers

Main Conveyor

Casting Conveyor

Conveyor

-------------------- Cut Here --------------------

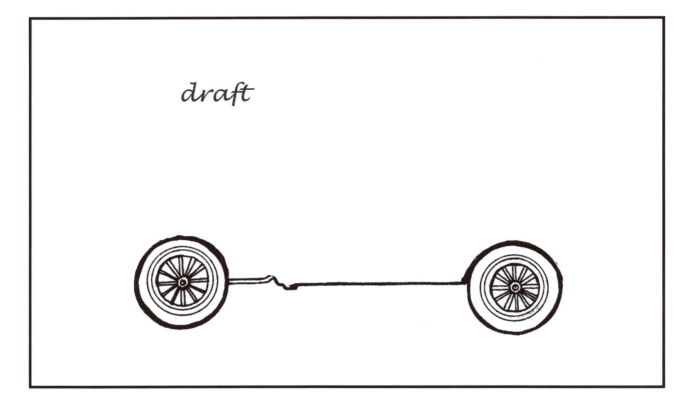

draft

Historical Background
Alexander Graham Bell

Born in Scotland in 1847, Alexander Graham Bell is best known for the invention of the telephone.

Bell's father worked as a teacher of those who were deaf and/or mute. Young Bell would often assist his father, eventually becoming a student teacher, and then he himself became a teacher of a class of deaf children. Innately interested in sound, Bell read a book describing experiments with tuning forks to make sounds. The book about acoustics, written by Hermann von Helmholtz, inspired Bell to telegraph speech.

In 1872, Bell began experimenting with the idea of sending several telegraph messages at a time. In 1874, he developed the idea for the telephone. However, Bell lacked the electrical knowledge to make the invention a reality. He found help at an electrical instrument shop. Thus, the partnership between Bell and Thomas Watson began.

Bell and Watson began experimenting with a harmonic telegraph. They thought that it could pick up the sound of the human voice. On March 7, 1876, Bell and Watson were given a patent. Success would follow three days later when they were able to transmit the human voice for the first time.

Bell and Watson went on to demonstrate their invention. The first telephone company, Bell Telephone Company, was founded July 9, 1877.

Bell died August 2, 1922.

Alexander Graham Bell Scene

Goal
- Recognize the accomplishments of Alexander Graham Bell
- Appreciate how this inventor changed the world

Description of Scene
This scene takes place at Bell's lab/workshop in Boston in early 1875, prior to his famous demonstration of the working telephone on June 2, 1875.

Clues
- Magnet, copper wire
- Experiment logbook (page 42)
- Table

Setting Up the Scene
Reserve an approximate 10' x 8' section of your classroom. Place all items on a table or another hard surface.

Higher Level Activities
Discussion Questions
- How did Bell's invention change from his first idea?

- Why was it important that Bell enlist the help of Thomas Watson?

- Do you think inventions happen sometimes by accident? Do you think the telephone was something of an accident? Have you ever thought of an invention by accident?

Follow-up Activities
- Have students list all of the items we now have because of the telephone.

- Have students imagine the consequences of a world in which the telephone did not exist.

- Have students create an advertisement promoting the telephone.

- The telephone replaced the telegraph. Have students brainstorm what they think could replace the telephone in the future.

- Have students create another clue that may have appeared in this scene.

Investigating the Scene

1. Your big question:
   Whose lab/workshop are you in?

2. Mark approximate time period on the time line below.

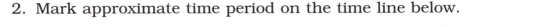

1800   1850   1900   1950   2000

3. List the clues you see in the scene. List important items about each clue (see page 10 *"How to Investigate Historical Clues"* for help).

4. What is your hypothesis about what is going on in the scene?

5. What do you need to know about each clue? List your smaller questions to help you answer the big question.

6. Research your final answer to the big question. Use *"Think About It"* to help you. Hint: The answers to your smaller questions will help you answer the big question.

7. Was your hypothesis correct?

8. What else do you want to know? List other questions you have about this historical topic.

- -

Think About It

This invention changed the world in all the ways except:

   A. Able to talk to people across distances
   B. Reduced need for letter writing
   C. Telegraph invention eventually not needed
   D. Delayed communication

What is another effect this invention has had upon the world? The effect can be either positive or negative.

_____

Provided Clues – Alexander Graham Bell

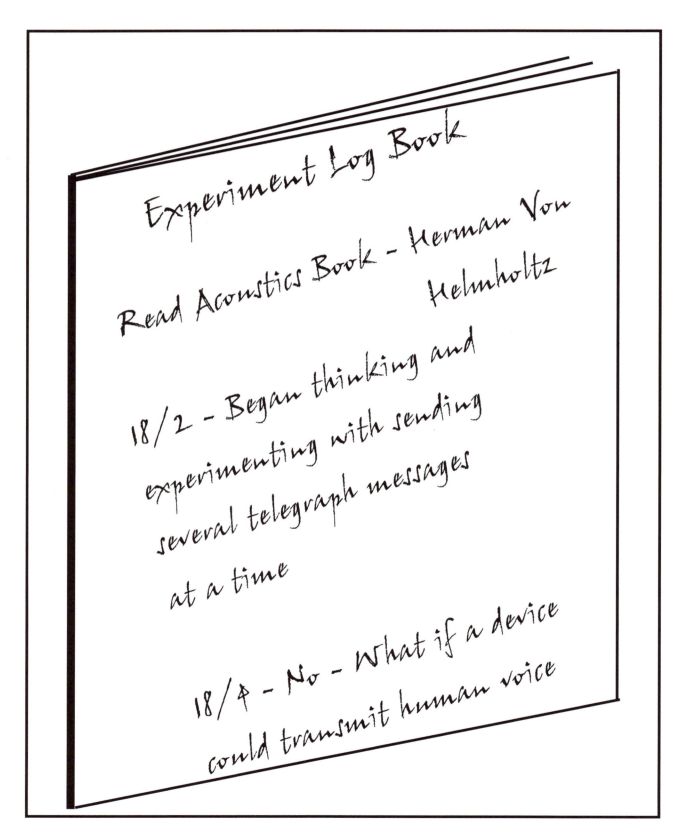

Experiment Log Book

Read Acoustics Book – Herman Von Helmholtz

18/2 – Began thinking and experimenting with sending several telegraph messages at a time

18/4 – No – What if a device could transmit human voice

Historical Background – Wright Brothers

Orville and Wilbur Wright will be forever known as the inventors of the first successful airplane. Sons of Bishop and Susan Wright, Wilbur was born in Indiana in 1867, while Orville was born in Dayton, Ohio, in 1871.

When they were in their twenties, the brothers rented and sold bicycles. Soon they began to build bicycles on their own.

In 1899, the Wright brothers began reading on the subject of flight – a subject they had been interested in for some time. They read all that was written on the subject including Otto Lilienthal's tables of air pressure on curved surfaces.

They constructed their first glider and wrote the Weather Bureau (now the National Weather Service) for suggestions as to where to test. Kitty Hawk, North Carolina, was the suggestion. Upon completing their test at Kitty Hawk, the Wright brothers reasoned that all published tables of air pressure on curved surfaces must be incorrect.

They returned to Dayton and constructed a wind tunnel at their bicycle shop. These experiments provided them with the data to make the first accurate tables of air pressure on curved surfaces.

In December of 1903, the Wright brothers tested a gasoline-powered machine at the Kitty Hawk location. The first airplane reached a speed of about 30 miles per hour. By 1908, the United States Department of War offered them a contract to build the first military airplane.

Wright Brothers Scene

Goal
- Recognize the accomplishments of the Wright brothers
- Appreciate how these inventors changed the world

Description of Scene
This scene takes place not long before the Wright brothers embarked on their test flight in Kitty Hawk, North Carolina. The location of this scene, however, is their bicycle shop in Dayton, Ohio. The scene takes place in early 1903, before their December 17 flight of that same year.

Clues
- Map – circling Kitty Hawk (page 46)
- Letter to Weather Bureau (page 46) – historical recreation
- Excerpt from the writings of Otto Lilienthal – can be found on the Internet. The Wright brothers read and ultimately disproved his air pressure tables.
- Fan – This clue simulates the wind tunnel the Wright brothers built in their bicycle shop.
- For effect, you may also have bicycle parts in the scene.

* A physical education teacher or coach may have a big fan you could use for this scene. Remind students that although the fan appears modern, they should imagine that it is much older.

Setting up the scene
Reserve an approximate 10' x 12' area of your classroom. Place the fan near the back of the scene. All other items may be placed on a table or hard surface.

<u>Higher Level Activities</u>
Discussion Questions
- Why was it important that the Wright brothers read Otto Lilienthal?
- Why was it important that they disagreed with Otto Lilienthal?
- Would you have flown their plane at Kitty Hawk? Why or why not?
- Why did these inventors need to write the Weather Bureau?

<u>Follow-up Activities</u>
- Have students list all of the items we now have because of the airplane.
- Have students imagine a world in which the airplane did not exist.
- Have students create an advertisement promoting the airplane.
- Have students brainstorm a list of pre-existing scientific ideas we now have. Then, hypothesize one that could be proven incorrect in the future.
- Have students create another clue that may have appeared in this scene.

Investigating the Scene

1. Your big question:
   Whose lab/workshop are you in?

2. Mark approximate time period on the time line below.

   1800   1850   1900   1950   2000

3. List the clues you see in the scene. List important items about each clue (see page 10 *"How to Investigate Historical Clues"* for help).

4. What is your hypothesis about what is going on in the scene?

5. What do you need to know about each clue? List your smaller questions to help you answer the big question.

6. Research your final answer to the big question. Use *"Think About It"* to help you. Hint: The answers to your smaller questions will help you answer the big question.

7. Was your hypothesis correct?

8. What else do you want to know? List other questions you have about this historical topic.

- -

Think About It

This invention changed the world in all the ways except:

   A. Get places much faster
   B. Help United States during wars
   C. Virtually reduce the need for trains and ships
   D. Reduced the need for metal, steel

What is another effect this invention has had upon the world? The effect can be either positive or negative.

_____

Provided Clues – Wright Brothers

May 13, 1900

Dear Weather Bureau,

-- Cut Here --

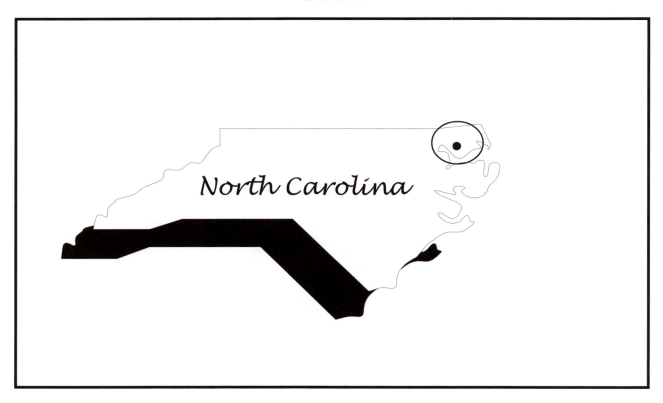

North Carolina

End of Chapter Activities

1. Compare and contrast inventors and inventions. Have students list all of the things you notice the inventors and the inventions have in common. Then list differences.

2. Have students invent a new school supply or improve upon an existing school supply. Students first design an experiment they would need to conduct, and then list the effects their invention would have upon the students, the teachers, and any other area.

3. Have students decide which invention has had the most profound effect upon society. Then write a newspaper editorial defending their choices.

4. Ask students to list problems yet to be solved. Then have students brainstorm an invention that solves the problem.

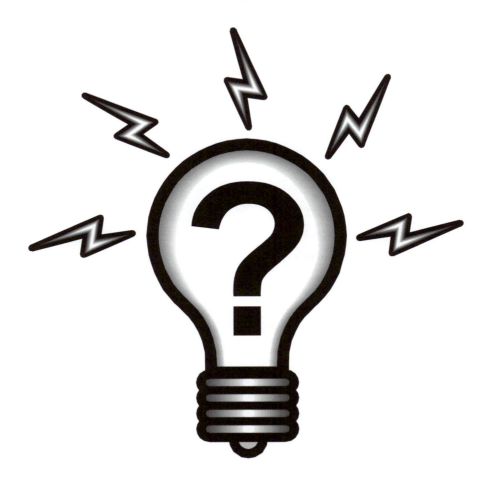

Chapter 4

Early Settlements

Historical Background – Jamestown

Carrying 105 passengers, the ships *Susan Constant*, *Godspeed*, and *Discovery* landed in what is now Chesapeake Bay, Virginia, on May 6, 1607. The passengers, sent by a group of London merchants known as the Virginia Company, were in search of treasure and were to spread Christianity among the Native Americans. Thus, the first permanent settlement, Jamestown, was formed on North American soil.

The first year of the settlement was plagued by disease because the new settlers were not educated in the ways of farming. Then, Captain John Smith became leader of the settlement and demanded that settlers work to provide food and shelter instead of looking for treasures. Smith remained in Jamestown for a year.

After Smith's departure, the settlement once again became plagued by disease, starvation, Indian attacks, and drought. Things would improve with the introduction of a new kind of tobacco by John Rolfe. Further, Rolfe discovered a new way of curing the leaves. This tobacco became very popular in Europe. Thus, a solid economic foundation was formed. Rolfe further contributed to the survival of Johnstown by marrying Pocahontas, the Indian princess. This marriage would bring about a peace, however short-lived, between the settlers and the Native Americans.

The first lawmaking assembly, consisting of representatives of the people, met in Jamestown. This legislative assembly was known as the House of Burgesses, and its operation created a framework for the future United States government.

Despite the many positive events, the Jamestown settlement would once again be vulnerable to attack first by the Indians then by a rebellion. These events would lead to the eventual demise of the settlement.

Jamestown Scene

Goal

- To recognize the reasons why the Jamestown settlers came to America
- To appreciate the challenges encountered by the Jamestown settlers

Description of Scene

The timing of this scene is in the years following the discovery of tobacco as a cash crop. This crop would ensure the survival of the settlement. The scene takes place in the home of a Jamestown settler.

Clues

- Tobacco or a substitute made to look like tobacco
- Records of events at Jamestown (page 53)

Setting Up the Scene

Reserve an approximate 8' x 10' area of your classroom. Place all clues on a table or another hard surface.

Higher Level Activities
Discussion Questions

- Do you think the settlers of Jamestown worked well together?

- What did the entry regarding looking for gold tell you about the motive of the settlers?

- What does this scene tell you about having strong leaders?

Follow-up Activities

- Have students compare/contrast Jamestown to a previously studied settlement. Students could show likenesses/differences through a Venn diagram, an essay, or a chart.

- Have students make a "scrapbook" of Jamestown. Their scrapbooks should contain illustrations with labels to provide a history of Jamestown.

- Have students imagine if the settlers had found a treasure at Jamestown. Students could compose an essay about how Jamestown and/ or America might be different.

- Have students brainstorm how they might have solved some of the problems encountered by the Jamestown settlers.

- Have students create another clue that may have appeared in the scene.

Investigating the Scene

1. Your big questions:

   a. **What early American settlement do these clues belong to?**

   b. **What challenges did they face and how did they overcome those challenges?**

2. Mark approximate time period on the time line below.

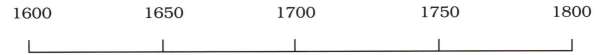

   1600   1650   1700   1750   1800

3. List the clues you see in the scene. List important items about each clue (see page 10 *"How to Investigate Historical Clues"* for help).

4. What is your hypothesis about what is going on in the scene?

5. What do you need to know about each clue? List your smaller questions to help you answer the bigger questions.

6. Research your final answer to the big questions. Use the *"Think About It"* page to help you. Hint: The answers to your smaller questions will help you answer the bigger questions.

7. Was your hypothesis correct?

8. What else do you want to know? List other questions you have about this historical topic.

Think About It

It could be ...(choose one)	**It could NOT be** ...(choose one)

It could be ...(choose one)

A. Plymouth

B. Massachusetts Bay Colony

C. Jamestown

.... because (mark the box next
to the reasons **WHY**)

❑ Located in the south

❑ Located in what is now
New England

❑ Made peace quickly with the
Native Americans and
considered them friends

It could NOT be ...(choose one)

A. Plymouth

B. Massachusetts Bay Colony

C. Jamestown

..... because (mark the box next
to the reasons **WHY NOT**)

❑ Located in the south

❑ Located in what is now
New England

❑ Made peace quickly with the
Native Americans and
considered them friends

Based upon the answers above, I think the clues belong to

_____ .

Provided Clues – Jamestown Settlement

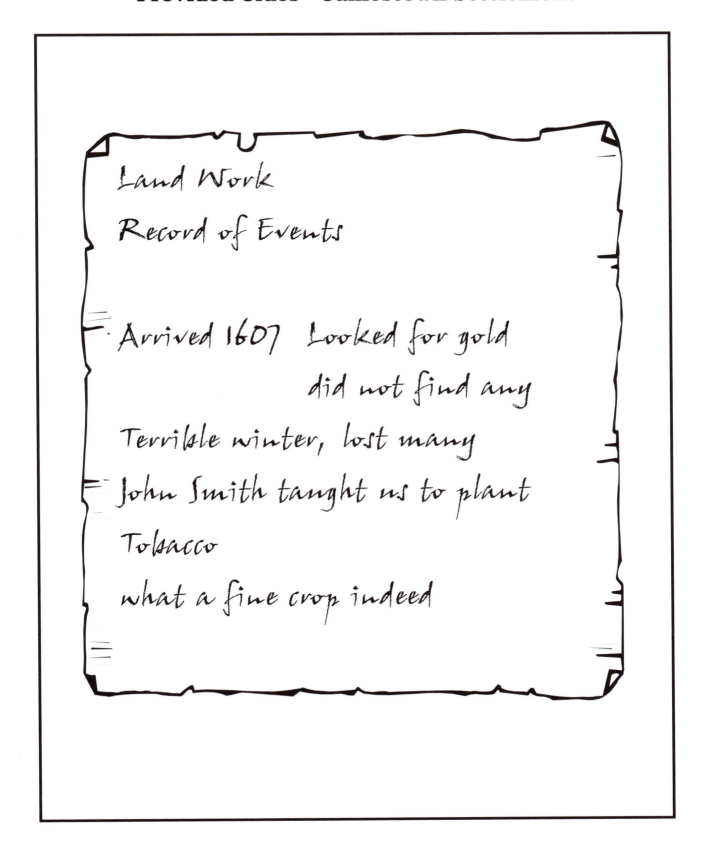

Land Work

Record of Events

Arrived 1607   Looked for gold

did not find any

Terrible winter, lost many

John Smith taught us to plant

Tobacco

what a fine crop indeed

Historical Background
Plymouth Colony

In search of religious freedom, a group known as the Pilgrims boarded a ship called the *Mayflower* to settle a new land – America. Thus, the second permanent settlement in North America was born on December 21, 1620. In what is now Massachusetts, the Pilgrims named their settlement Plymouth.

Not only did the Pilgrims bring with them their ideals for religious freedom, they also initiated the notion that the people could govern themselves through such actions as the Mayflower Compact and electing a governor, John Carver. Because they were going to an area without discipline or authority, the Pilgrims solved this problem through the Compact, which outlined the expectations of behavior in the new land. The Pilgrim ideals of religious freedom and self-government helped set the framework for what would become the United States.

Despite overcoming the challenge of the absence of authority, the Pilgrims encountered harsh conditions in the new land including a harsh winter that would claim half of their residents. Further, the Pilgrims had little success in the area of farming. Fortunately, the Pilgrims made friends with the Native Americans, one of which was Squanto, who taught them to catch alewives fish. This kind of fish is also used as a fertilizer in planting beans, pumpkins, and corn. Squanto's teachings would ultimately allow the settlement to flourish prompting Governor William Bradford to call for a celebration in 1621. The feast was a three-day celebration that included their Native American friends.

Ultimately, the Plymouth settlement would flourish. Enough food would be grown to not only feed the citizens but also establish trade with other nations and colonies. Further, the ideals of religious freedom and self-government would instill harmony and productivity among its citizens.

Plymouth Scene

Goal
- To recognize the reasons why the Pilgrims came to America
- To appreciate the challenges encountered by the Pilgrims

Description of Scene
The scene is the home of a Pilgrim family. The father has kept a diary of events that have happened in the past year including the loss of his wife and the eventual harvest celebration due to Squanto showing the Pilgrims how to plant. The scene takes place in 1621 just before the celebration.

Clues
- Dirt and seeds – these clues are in the scene to show that the Pilgrims had learned to fertilize their crops
- Diary entry (page 58) – this clue is in the scene to show how things changed for the Pilgrims in terms of survival of the settlement
- A copy of the Mayflower Compact can be found on the Internet
- Candle – this clue is to establish the time period
- Ears of corn, pumpkins – may also be in the scene to show that food was now available and a feast was pending
- Native American feathers, jewelry, etc. – this shows that the settlers were on friendly terms with the Native Americans, even exchanging gifts

Setting Up the Scene
Place the diary entry, the Mayflower Compact, feather pen, the candle, the pumpkins, the corn, and Native American items all on the table or another hard surface.

<u>Higher Level Activities</u>
Discussion Questions
- How did things change for the Pilgrims in just one year?
- Why did things change?
- What does this scene tell you about working together?
- Why was the Mayflower Compact necessary?

<u>Follow-up Activities</u>
- Have students compare/contrast Jamestown to a previously studied settlement. Students could show likenesses/differences through a Venn diagram, an essay, or a chart.
- With the Mayflower Compact as inspiration, have students imagine that all the school authority disappeared and that it was now incumbent upon them to create their own self-government.
- Have students replace some of the values and beliefs of Plymouth Colony with those of another colony.
- Have students pretend they are producing a Hollywood movie about the first year of the Plymouth settlement. They should come up with a movie title and design a movie poster.
- Have students create another clue that may have appeared in the scene.

Investigating the Scene

1. Your big questions:

   a. What early American settlement do these clues belong to?

   b. What challenges did they face and how did they overcome those challenges?

2. Mark approximate time period on the time line below.

   1600   1650   1700   1750   1800

   └────────────┴────────────┴────────────┴────────────┘

3. List the clues you see in the scene. List important items about each clue (see page 10 *"How to Investigate Historical Clues"* for help).

4. What is your hypothesis about what is going on in the scene?

5. What do you need to know about each clue? List your smaller questions to help you answer the bigger questions.

6. Research your final answer to the big questions. Use the *"Think About It"* page to help you. Hint: The answers to your smaller questions will help you answer the bigger questions.

7. Was your hypothesis correct?

8. What else do you want to know? List other questions you have about this historical topic.

Think About It

It could be ...(choose one)

A. Plymouth

B. Massachusetts Bay Colony

C. Jamestown

.... because (mark the box next to the reasons **WHY**)

❑ Located in the south

❑ Located in what is now New England

❑ Set up a democratic government

❑ Made peace quickly with the Native Americans and considered them friends

It could NOT be ...(choose one)

A. Plymouth

B. Massachusetts Bay Colony

C. Jamestown

..... because (mark the box next to the reasons **WHY NOT**)

❑ Not located in the south

❑ Not located in what is now New England

❑ Not many left the settlement because of disagreements

❑ Did not make peace quickly with the Native Americans and did not consider them friends

Based upon the answers above, I think the clues belong to

_____ .

Provided Clues – Plymouth Colony

Dear Diary,

On the eve of a great celebration called by our governor Bradford, I must take this time to reflect upon my life in the new country.

How I miss my dear wife. That first winter was dreadful. Help was on the way with Squanto's alewives fish! If only she could have hung on. She will certainly be with me tomorrow as we celebrate.

Historical Background – Massachusetts Bay Colony

On a quest to establish a "perfect society," a group from England known as the Puritans fled their native land. There they had been persecuted for their religious beliefs that differed from the Anglican Church. Arriving in 1630, near what is now Boston Bay, the Puritans would help establish the Massachusetts Bay Colony.

Denise Plumlee-Tadlock

Life in Puritan Massachusetts left little personal freedom. Each Puritan was required to attend the Puritan Congregational Church. Because of the Puritans' strict interpretation of the Bible, the Church intervened in most civil matters including issues between a parent and child. Because it was considered a sin, it was also a crime in Puritan society to dance, drink, or argue on Sunday. Clearly, there was no separation of church and state. Further, the Puritan leadership failed to set up a representative government. For all of these reasons, many Puritans became weary of living under the rigid conditions.

Several Puritans would be banished from Puritan Massachusetts for publicly objecting to Puritan beliefs. Roger Williams, banished in 1635, would establish the colony of Rhode Island. Anne Hutchinson, one of the few women who could read and write, held discussion groups in her home criticizing the Puritan minister. She, too, was banished.

Because of the intolerant rules, the English government would eventually take over Massachusetts making it a Royal Colony.

Massachusetts Bay Colony Scene

Goal
- To recognize the values dictating the Puritan settlement
- To recognize the problems that would arise from said values

Description of Scene
The scene is a home of a male Puritan following the banishment of Roger Williams. This person is contemplating leaving with Williams. The scene takes place in 1635, in Massachusetts Bay Colony.

Clues
- A map marking the Rhode Island territory (page 63) – this clue exists to show that the person is leaving Massachusetts
- Bag/luggage – to show that the person is leaving
- Candle – to establish the time period
- Feather pen – to establish the time period
- Black and white clothes – to show that the person may be packing

Higher Level Activities
Discussion Questions
- Why did people leave Massachusetts Bay Colony?

- How did the Puritans define a "perfect society?"

- When you think about why the Puritans came to America, what is interesting about why many left the settlement?

Follow-up Activities
- Have students compare and contrast the Massachusetts Bay Colony to a previously studied settlement. Students could show likenesses and differences through a Venn diagram, essay, or a chart.

- Have students imagine if people had not left the Massachusetts Bay Colony. How would America be different today? Students could compose an essay or share their answers orally.

- Have students design a travel brochure promoting the Colony of Rhode Island to the remaining Puritans.

- Have students brainstorm a list of ways the Puritan leaders could have kept the settlement together.

- Have students create another clue that may have appeared in this scene.

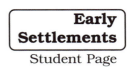

Investigating the Scene

1. Your big questions:

    a. What early American settlement do these clues belong to?

    b. Is this person happy with the settlement?

2. Mark approximate time period on the time line below.

    1600   1650   1700   1750   1800

3. List the clues you see in the scene. List important items about each clue (see page 10 ***"How to Investigate Historical Clues"*** for help).

4. What is your hypothesis about what is going on in the scene?

5. What do you need to know about each clue? List your smaller questions to help you answer the bigger questions.

6. Research your final answer to the big questions. Use the ***"Think About It"*** page to help you. Hint: The answers to your smaller questions will help you answer the bigger questions.

7. Was your hypothesis correct?

8. What else do you want to know? List other questions you have about this historical topic.

Think About It

It could be ...(choose one)	**It could NOT be** ...(choose one)

It could be ...(choose one)

A. Plymouth

B. Massachusetts Bay Colony

C. Jamestown

.... because (mark the box next to the reasons **WHY**)

❑ Located in the south

❑ Located in what is now New England

❑ Set up a democratic government

❑ Made peace quickly with the Native Americans and considered them friends

It could NOT be ...(choose one)

A. Plymouth

B. Massachusetts Bay Colony

C. Jamestown

..... because (mark the box next to the reasons **WHY NOT**)

❑ Located in the south

❑ Located in what is now New England

❑ Set up a democratic government

❑ Made peace quickly with the Native Americans and considered them friends

Based upon the answers above, I think the clues belong to

_____.

Provided Clues – Massachusetts Colony

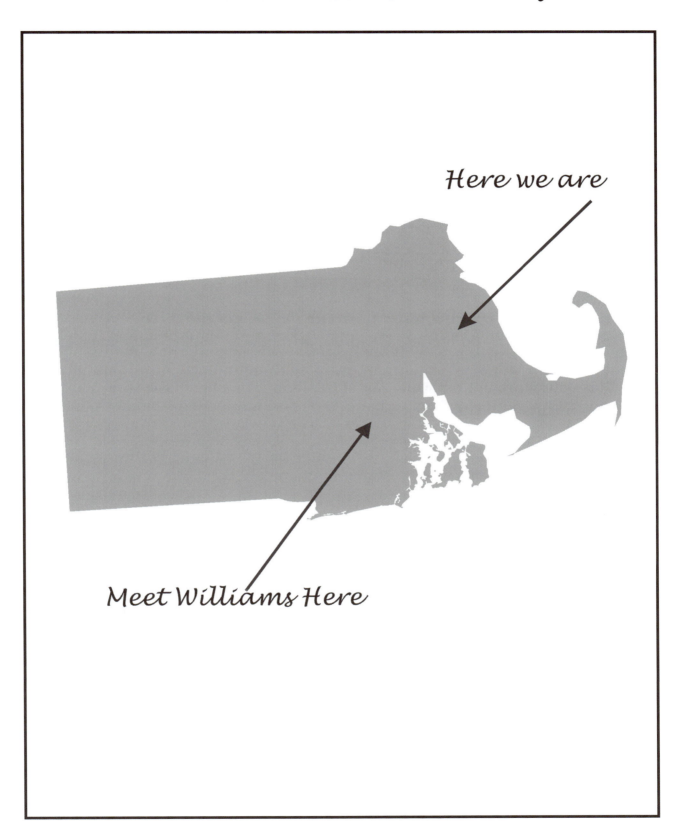

Here we are

Meet Williams Here

End of Chapter Activities

1. Have students compare/contrast the three early American settlements. Show likenesses and differences through a chart.

2. Have students make a model settlement. They can construct this settlement or it could be drawn on paper. Have students pretend they are setting up a colony on Mars and must establish a type of government, economy, housing, etc. Students need to research Mars to complete this activity.

3. Have students write a letter of advice to members of one of the three settlements.

4. Have students create a travel brochure for each of the three early settlements. Items could include location, "attractions," rules/guidelines, etc.

5. Have students brainstorm a list of the long-term effects the three early settlements had upon America.

6. Have students debate which of the three early settlements they would have liked to live in.

Chapter 5

Native Americans

Setting Up Native American Scenes
Directions For Teachers

1. Select the Native American tribe you would like your students to study. This may be pre-determined by your state/local curriculum.

2. Divide students into groups of four. Assign each group a Native American tribe.

3. Explain to students that they are going to research their assigned tribe and then set up a scene challenging other groups to figure out their assigned tribe based upon clues in the scene. Instruct students that their scene should appear like their particular tribe's village might have appeared.

4. Provide each group with an allotted amount of space. This space may be dependent upon the size of your classroom. Generally, a 5' x 8' area would be ideal.

5. Review the provided student activity sheet. This activity sheet provides students with a template showing how to set up their Native American scene.

6. Once students set up their scenes, they may then investigate the other groups' scenes (see "Investigating Native American Scene Activity Sheet"). The investigation will be similar to the way in which scenes in previous chapters are conducted. You may want to provide students with a list of all tribes studied.

Other Recommendations

Because students are setting up their own scenes, it is important that they have investigated at least one scene from the previous chapters. You may want to number each scene once they are completed to better manage the activity.

Since students will be investigating more than one scene, you may want to make multiple copies of the "Investigating the Native American Scene Activity Sheet" as this sheet can be used for one investigation only.

Follow-Up Activities

- Have students compare/contrast the Native American tribes using a chart showing likenesses and differences.

- Have students make up a card or board game about the studied Native American tribes.

- Have students make a crossword puzzle about the Native American tribes.

- Have students combine two or more tribes to create a new tribe.

- Have students brainstorm the long-term effects that Native Americans have had upon the region in which they lived.

Setting Up A Native American Scene
Activity Sheet

1. The tribe your group was assigned _____.

2. Gather research on the following areas about your assigned tribe.

    - Housing
    - Customs/Traditions
    - History – was your tribe involved in any wars or conflicts?
    - Geographic area in which the tribe lived
    - Leadership
    - Other things that make your tribe special

3. After researching, brainstorm clues you might have in the scene about the areas you researched. Try not to make the clues too obvious. Remember, you want to challenge your classmates! For instance, if you discover your tribe made pottery, you could have clay instead of having a pottery piece in the scene.

4. Once you have decided on the clues, then it is time to set up your scene. Your group should set up the scene as if the investigator is walking into the Native American's village. Your scene will not be the entire village – just enough to fill the space your teacher allows. It may help to draw a picture or diagram before your group sets up the scene.

	Information	Possible clue
Housing		
Customs, traditions		
History		
Geographic area		
Leadership		
Other things that make your tribe special		

5. Make or gather your clues.

Investigating the
Native American Scene

1. Your big question:
   Which tribe do these clues belong to?

2. Mark approximate time period on the time line below.

__00   __50   __00   __50   __00

3. List the clues you see in the scene. List important items about each clue (see page 10 ***"How to Investigate Historical Clues"*** for help).

4. What is your hypothesis about what is going on in the scene?

5. What do you need to know about each clue? List your smaller questions to help you answer the big question.

6. Research your final answer to the big question. Hint: The answers to your smaller questions will help you answer the big question.

7. Was your hypothesis correct?

8. What else do you want to know? List other questions you have about this historical topic.

Chapter 6

Government

Branches of Government –
Historical Background

When the architects of the United States Constitution met to draft this historical document, they had learned the lessons of the past. No one person or entity (hence a king) should have ultimate power. Division of power would avoid tyranny. Thus, the powers of government were divided into three branches: the Legislative, the Executive, and the Judicial. This system allows for balance of power and checks and balances – each branch may check on one another.

- **The Executive Branch**

  The primary function is to carry out the laws. Persons in this branch are executives: the President, governors, and mayors. The Executive Branch can sign or veto laws and can appoint judges.

- **The Legislative Branch**

  The primary function is to write and pass laws. Persons in this branch are senators and congressmen/congresswomen. Congress can override Presidents' vetoes.

- **The Judicial Branch**

  The primary function of this branch is to interpret the laws. Persons in this branch of government are judges, police officers, and others involved in law enforcement. The Supreme Court, the highest court, can rule that laws are unconstitutional and can declare a President's actions unconstitutional.

  Except for some judges who are appointed, the people elect all of these people. In this representative democracy, these people elected to either the Executive, Legislative, or Judicial Branch are elected by the people.

Legislative Branch Scene

Goal

- To recognize the duties/powers of the Legislative Branch

Description of Scene

Note: Before this scene, explain that a law is called a "bill" before it is voted on to become a law.

The scene takes place in the office of a legislator about to make decisions about whether to vote for upcoming legislation, and also the legislator is working on writing a law.

Clues

- Incomplete law (page 74)
- Manila file titled "Law in Process"
- "To Do List" (page 74)
- Desk – to hold clues
- For effect, you may have office supplies on the desk.

Setting Up The Scene

Place all of the items on a desk or another hard surface.

Investigating the Scene

1. Your big question:
   Which branch of government does this person belong to?

2. Mark approximate time period on the time line below.

   1850   1900   1950   2000   2050
   └───────────┴───────────┴───────────┴───────────┘

3. List the clues you see in the scene. List important items about each clue (see page 10 **"How to Investigate Historical Clues"** for help).

4. What is your hypothesis about what is going on in the scene?

5. What do you need to know about each clue? List your smaller questions to help you answer the big question.

6. Research your final answer to the big question. Use the **"Think About It"** page to help you. Hint: The answers to your smaller questions will help you answer the big question.

7. Was your hypothesis correct?

8. What else do you want to know? List other questions you have about this historical topic.

Think About It

Think about why the clues in the scene could **NOT** belong to a particular branch. Then choose the two branches that it could **NOT** be and write a paragraph defending your choices.

Executive

_____

_____

_____

_____

Legislative

_____

_____

_____

_____

Judicial

_____

_____

_____

_____

Provided Clues – Legislative Branch

Rough draft of law

Every person must report all neighborhood animal related abuse to local authorities

--- Cut Here ---

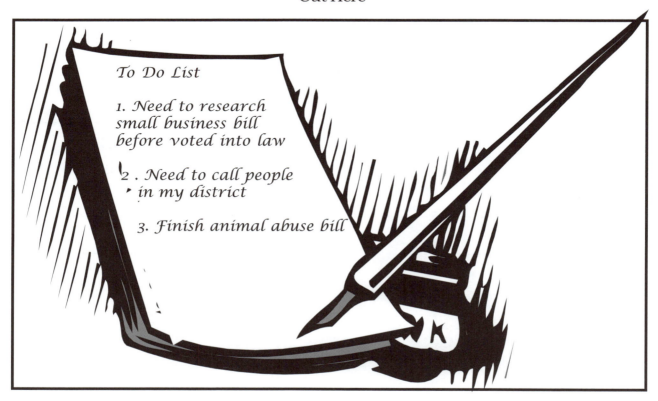

To Do List

1. Need to research small business bill before voted into law

2. Need to call people in my district

3. Finish animal abuse bill

Executive Branch Scene

Goal

- To recognize the duties/powers of the Executive Branch

Description of Scene

The scene takes place in the office of an executive who has just vetoed and signed laws.

Clues

- Signed law (page 78)
- Vetoed law (page 78)
- Desk
- For effect, you may have office supplies on the desk.

Setting Up The Scene

Place all items on the desk or another hard surface.

Investigating the Scene

1. Your big question:
   Which branch of government does this person belong to?

2. Mark approximate time period on the time line below.

   1850   1900   1950   2000   2050

   |_____|_____|_____|_____|

3. List the clues you see in the scene. List important items about each clue (see page 10 *"How to Investigate Historical Clues"* for help).

4. What is your hypothesis about what is going on in the scene?

5. What do you need to know about each clue? List your smaller questions to help you answer the big question.

6. Research your final answer to the big question. Use the *"Think About It"* page to help you. Hint: The answers to your smaller questions will help you answer the big question.

7. Was your hypothesis correct?

8. What else do you want to know? List other questions you have about this historical topic.

Think About It

Think about why the clues in the scene could **NOT** belong to a particular branch. Then choose the two branches that it could **NOT** be and write a paragraph defending your choices.

Executive

_____

_____

_____

_____

Legislative

_____

_____

_____

_____

Judicial

_____

_____

_____

_____

Provided Clues – Executive Branch

Clean Air Law
Passed by Congress

Catherine Jones
signed

_____
vetoed

-- Cut Here Line --

Post Offices open 24 hours
Law passed by Congress

_____
signed

Catherine Jones
vetoed

Judicial Branch Scene

Goal

- To recognize the duties/powers of the Judicial Branch

Description of Scene

The scene takes place in a judge's chambers. The judge is about to make a decision on a court case.

Clues

- Law books **
- Notes on trial (page 82) **
- Desk – to hold items
- For effect, you may have office supplies on the desk.

** These clues exist to show that the judge is attempting to interpret the law in making his/her decision.

Setting Up The Scene

Place all of the items on a desk or another hard surface.

Investigating the Scene

1. Your big question:
   Which branch of government does this person belong to?

2. Mark approximate time period on the time line below.

   1850   1900   1950   2000   2050

3. List the clues you see in the scene. List important items about each clue (see page 10 ***"How to Investigate Historical Clues"*** for help).

4. What is your hypothesis about what is going on in the scene?

5. What do you need to know about each clue? List your smaller questions to help you answer the big question.

6. Research your final answer to the big question. Use the ***"Think About It"*** page to help you. Hint: The answers to your smaller questions will help you answer the big question.

7. Was your hypothesis correct?

8. What else do you want to know? List other questions you have about this historical topic.

Think About It

Think about why the clues in the scene could **NOT** belong to a particular branch. Then choose the two branches that it could **NOT** be and write a paragraph defending your choices.

Executive

_____

_____

_____

_____

Legislative

_____

_____

_____

_____

Judicial

_____

_____

_____

_____

Provided Clues – Judicial Branch

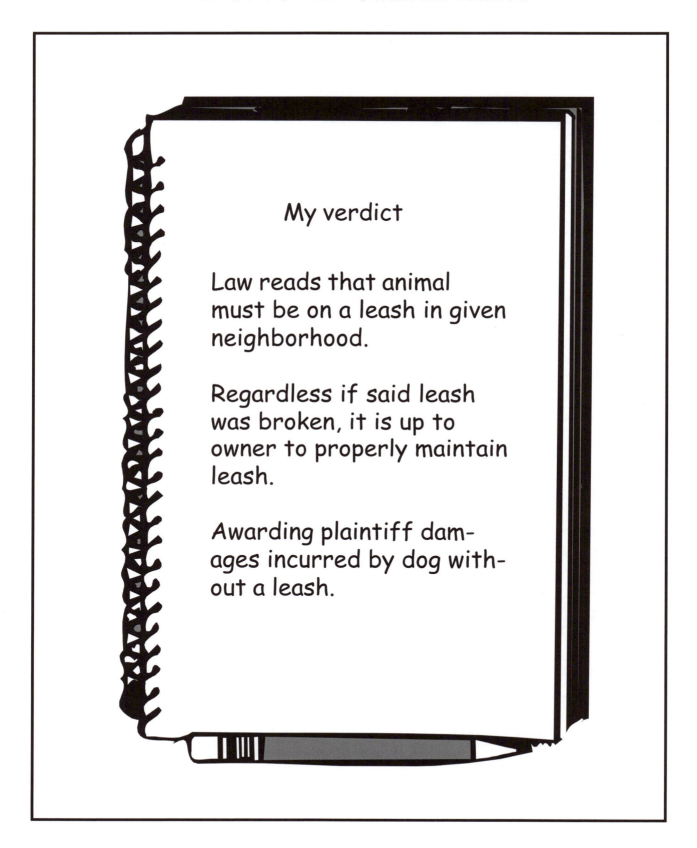

My verdict

Law reads that animal must be on a leash in given neighborhood.

Regardless if said leash was broken, it is up to owner to properly maintain leash.

Awarding plaintiff damages incurred by dog without a leash.

End of Chapter Activities

Discussion Questions

1. Why is it important that the people elect those individuals in the branches of government?

2. Which branch do you think is the most important? Explain your answer.

3. Which branch has the most people? Why? Which has the least? Why?

Follow-Up Activities

1. Have students combine two branches of government to make one new branch of government. What would this new branch be called? What would its powers be?

2. Have students relate the branches of government to how other establishments in their lives operate – school or their own household.

3. Have students create a balance of power chart. Create three columns. In each column, list the branch of government and its duties. Draw arrows to items showing the balance of power. For instance, an arrow would be drawn from "President can veto" to "Congress can override a veto."

4. Divide students into the three branches of government. The Legislative Branch will write and pass laws. The Executive Branch will sign or veto those laws and the Judicial Branch will interpret the laws. The laws should involve the classroom.

5. Create another clue that may have appeared in each of the three scenes.

6. In a writing assignment or class discussion, have students imagine that these branches did not exist. How would the U.S. be different?

7. Brainstorm how they might improve the branches of government.

Chapter 7

Citizenship

Historical Background –
American Flag/Betsy Ross

Born Elizabeth Griscom on January 1, 1752, in Philadelphia, Pennsylvania, Betsy Ross as a youth would be apprenticed to a local upholsterer. There, Betsy met another apprentice, John Ross. They married and soon opened their own upholstery business.

As the American Revolution drew near, John Ross joined the Philadelphia militia. While on duty in mid-January of 1776, he was wounded by an explosion and later died.

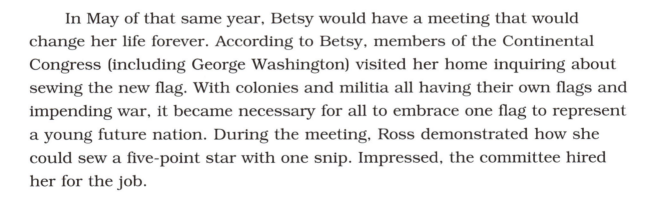

In May of that same year, Betsy would have a meeting that would change her life forever. According to Betsy, members of the Continental Congress (including George Washington) visited her home inquiring about sewing the new flag. With colonies and militia all having their own flags and impending war, it became necessary for all to embrace one flag to represent a young future nation. During the meeting, Ross demonstrated how she could sew a five-point star with one snip. Impressed, the committee hired her for the job.

The new flag would have 13 stars and stripes to represent the thirteen colonies. As the nation grew so would the number of stars. Further, laws of etiquette would be written with regard to the maintenance and display of the American Flag.

Betsy Ross Scene

Goals
- To recognize the contributions of Betsy Ross
- To appreciate the importance of the American Flag

Description of Scene
This scene is shortly after Betsy Ross had her famous meeting with George Washington and other members of the Continental Congress. The scene takes place in early 1776, in Philadelphia, Pennsylvania.

Clues
- Scissors – this clue indicates the person was a seamstress
- Thread – this clue indicates the person was a seamstress
- Construction-paper flag (or made of cloth, if possible) containing 13 stripes and 13 stars – this clue helps establish the time period and how the first flag appeared
- Table – to hold clues
- Candle – to establish the time period

Setting Up the Scene
Set up an approximate 8' x 10' area. Place all clues on a table, desk, or other hard surface.

Higher Level Activities
Discussion Questions
- Why was there a need for a new flag?

- Why didn't the Flag in the scene have fifty stars?

Follow-up Activities
- Have students imagine if the members of the Continental Congress would have predicted that America would expand to fifty states. Students could propose an alternative design.

- Have students compare/contrast the United States Flag to the flags of other countries. How are they alike or different? Students could show likenesses and differences through a chart, Venn diagram, or an essay.

- Have students write a letter to Betsy Ross explaining to her what the Flag means to us today.

- Have students create another clue that may have appeared in this scene.

- Have students imagine a country with several flags and not one central American Flag. How would that affect the citizens?

Investigating the Scene

1. Your big questions:

   a. To whom do these clues belong?

   b. Why are they important?

2. Mark approximate time period on the time line below.

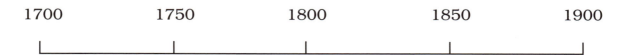

3. List the clues you see in the scene. List important items about each clue (see page 10 *"How to Investigate Historical Clues"* for help).

4. What is your hypothesis about what is going on in the scene?

5. What do you need to know about each clue? List your smaller questions to help you answer the bigger questions.

6. Research your final answer to the big questions. Use the *"Think About It"* page to help you. Hint: The answers to your smaller questions will help you answer the bigger questions.

7. Was your hypothesis correct?

8. What else do you want to know? List other questions you have about this historical topic.

Think About It

It could be ...(choose one)   **It could NOT be** ...(choose one)

A. Francis Scott Key

B. Betsy Ross

C. Benjamin Franklin

D. Thomas Jefferson

A. Francis Scott Key

B. Betsy Ross

C. Benjamin Franklin

D. Thomas Jefferson

.... because (mark the box next to the reasons **WHY**)

..... because (mark the box next to the reasons **WHY NOT**)

❑ The person lived during that time

❑ The person had written books or poems

❑ The person participated in the American Revolution

❑ The person had lived in Philadelphia

❑ The person did not live during that time

❑ The person was not a writer of books or poems

❑ The person did not participate in the American Revolution

❑ The person had not lived in Philadelphia

Based upon the answers above, I think the clues belong to

_____.

Historical Background –
The National Anthem/Francis Scott Key

Francis Scott Key wrote the Star Spangled Banner, now the United States national anthem, during the War of 1812. Originally a poem, Key later developed the music from an English song "To Anacreon in Heaven."

Born in Fredrick County, Maryland, in 1779, Key would become an influential Washington lawyer. Because of his influence, President James Madison granted him permission to obtain the release of his friend William Beanes from the British who had captured him during the War of 1812. In 1814, Key joined a U.S. Flag of truce ship. During this trip, Key became an eyewitness to the British attack of Fort McHenry in Baltimore Harbor. The attack lingered throughout the night. When morning arrived, Key observed that "our flag was still there" despite the devastating attack. His observation inspired him to write "The Star Spangled Banner."

In 1931, Congress formally adopted "The Star Spangled Banner" as the United States national anthem.

Francis Scott Key Scene

Goals
- To recognize the origin of our national anthem
- To recognize the significance of U.S. symbols, including the American flag and the sacrifice of those defending our country

Description of Scene
The scene is the room in which Key witnessed the Flag the morning after the Battle of Fort McHenry. The room was very tight quarters as Key was on a ship at the time of witnessing the attack. The scene takes place in the year 1814.

Clues
- Notes on "The Star Spangled Banner" (page 93) – this clue is to establish the activities of Key
- Illustration of what Key saw through a window (page 93) – this sight, according to history, inspired him to write "The Star Spangled Banner"
- A window or made-up window – Key observed the Flag through a window
- Ink jar – this clue helps establish the time period as well as show that the person was writing
- Feather pen – this clue helps establish the time period as well as show that the person was writing
- Small desk – this clue is part of the room where Key stayed on the ship

Setting Up the Scene
Reserve a 5' x 8' area of your classroom. Place the notes, feather pen, and ink jar all on the desk. Tape the illustration of the Flag onto the window prop. The Flag should appear in the distance, as Key would have observed.

Higher Level Activities
Discussion Questions
- Has a historical event inspired you to write a song or poem? If so, what event was it?
- Why do you think "The Star Spangled Banner" became so popular with Americans?
- Why do you think the Flag inspires people?
- How do you feel when you hear the song "The Star Spangled Banner?"

Follow-up Activities
- Have students compare/contrast "The Star Spangled Banner" to other songs with an American theme. Complete the activity with a Venn diagram, essay, or chart.
- Have students write a letter to Congress urging them to adopt "The Star Spangled Banner" as our national anthem. Remind students that the letter would have been written prior to 1931, and they should provide reasons why the song should be adopted.
- Have students create another clue that may have appeared in this scene.
- Have students substitute another historical event for the Battle of Fort McHenry and write another version of "The Star Spangled Banner."

Investigating the Scene

1. Your big questions:

   a. To whom do these clues belong?

   b. Why are they important?

2. Mark approximate time period on the time line below.

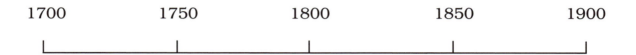

| 1700 | 1750 | 1800 | 1850 | 1900 |

3. List the clues you see in the scene. List important items about each clue (see page 10 ***"How to Investigate Historical Clues"*** for help).

4. What is your hypothesis about what is going on in the scene?

5. What do you need to know about each clue? List your smaller questions to help you answer the bigger questions.

6. Research your final answer to the big questions. Use the ***"Think About It"*** page to help you. Hint: The answers to your smaller questions will help you answer the bigger questions.

7. Was your hypothesis correct?

8. What else do you want to know? List other questions you have about this historical topic.

Think About It

It could be ...(choose one)   **It could NOT be** ...(choose one)

A. Francis Scott Key   A. Francis Scott Key

B. Betsy Ross   B. Betsy Ross

C. Benjamin Franklin   C. Benjamin Franklin

D. Thomas Jefferson   D. Thomas Jefferson

.... because (mark the box next   ..... because (mark the box next
to the reasons **WHY**)   to the reasons **WHY NOT**)

❑ The person lived during   ❑ The person did not live
that time   during that time

❑ The person had written   ❑ The person was not a writer
books or poems   of books or poems

❑ The person participated in   ❑ The person did not participate
the American Revolution   in the American Revolution

❑ The person had lived in   ❑ The person had not lived in
Philadelphia   Philadelphia

Based upon the answers above, I think the clues belong to

_____.

Clues Provided – The National Anthem
Francis Scott Key

Ft. McHenry – Oh say can you
see – rockets red glare
the flag's still there
star spangled

------------------------------- Cut Here -------------------------------

Historical Background – Voting

Voting is a means by which people decide on issues such as leaders and public-related items like building schools. The United States is a democracy and allows its citizens the right to vote unlike other nations that do not have a democracy and, therefore, the people do not choose their leaders.

Despite the democracy enjoyed today, the United States has evolved from humble beginnings as a "child" to its mother country England to a nation of its own. When the United States was ruled by England, its leader was a king. A king is a person who is born into power and maintains most decision-making authority. The citizens of the colonies did not agree with many of the King's decisions and on July 4, 1776, declared its independence from England.

Once the colonies (now the United States) obtained freedom from England, a Constitution was written that set up the United States government (including voting privileges). When the Constitution was initially written, only men could vote. The U.S. Constitution has since been amended several times to include women, people of race, and to lower the voting age to 18.

Further, the United States is no longer governed by a king. Leaders are instead elected by the people.

Voting Scene

Goals

- To demonstrate the habits of those who utilize good citizenship and vote
- To demonstrate the struggle of those before us in establishing a democracy

Description of Scene

The scene is the home of an American individual devoted to carrying out their civic duty of voting. The scene is set in modern America.

Clues

- Calendar marked on the second Tuesday of November (if possible, obtain an even-year calendar) – this clue shows that voting day is important to the person in the scene
- Letter from father to son (page 98) – this clue provides historical details regarding voting
- Newspaper (page 98) – this clue shows that the individual in the scene is trying to become informed of the issues prior to voting

Setting Up the Scene

All items should be placed on a desk except for the calendar, which should be hung nearby.

Higher Level Activities
Discussion Questions

- Do you agree with the father's reasons for encouraging his son to vote? If you could add a reason, what would it be?

- Do you think all Americans vote? How could more Americans be encouraged to vote?

- What are some effects of many people having the right to vote?

- Why do you think the father called voting a "duty?"

- Why did the father point out that we have a president and not a king?

Follow-up Activities

- Have students compare/contrast voting rights to driving rights. This activity could be an essay, chart, or Venn diagram.

- Have students defend in a speech or an essay whether they believe voting rights should be extended to 12-year-olds.

- Have students create another clue that may have appeared in this scene (see page 10 for help).

Investigating the Scene

1. Your big question:
   What do the clues in this scene tell you about how this person feels about voting?

2. Mark approximate time period on the time line below.

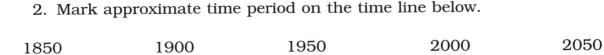

3. List the clues you see in the scene. List important items about each clue (see page 10 *"How to Investigate Historical Clues"* for help).

4. What is your hypothesis about what is going on in the scene?

5. What do you need to know about each clue? List your smaller questions to help you answer the big question.

6. Research your final answer to the big question. Use the *"Think About It"* page to help you. Hint: The answers to your smaller questions will help you answer the big question.

7. Was your hypothesis correct?

8. What else do you want to know? List other questions you have about this historical topic.

Think About It

Which of the following statements is more likely?

- A person is having trouble deciding which king to vote for.
- A person is having trouble deciding which person to vote for as president.

If this person did **NOT** believe voting was important, how might each of the clues be different?

The calendar

_____

_____

_____

_____

The diary entry/the letter

_____

_____

_____

_____

The newspaper

_____

_____

_____

_____

Clues Provided - Voting

Dear Son,

Now that you have reached your 18th birthday, you will now be blessed with your duty of voting. I wanted to share with you some reasons why this is so important:

1. You have ancestors who fought in the American Revolution for a free country. We now have a president and not a king as head of state.

2. Voting allows you to express your opinion on issues and who will lead the country.

Here are some important items from history for you to know:

July 4, 1776

Amendments 15, 19, and 26 to the United States Constitution

A little history lesson for you, Son.

Love,
Your Father

-- Cut Here ---- ---

THE SMALLVILLE TIMES

Candidates For Mayor To Debate
Wednesday Night At 7:30
Here is a brief look at how the candidates stand on certain issues:

<u>John Smith believes</u>   <u>Mary Powell believes</u>
Build new schools   Update current schools

Historical Background – Benjamin Franklin

Born in Boston on January 17, 1706, Benjamin Franklin could perhaps be considered one of America's greatest citizens. His greatness would include political, scientific, and philosophical contributions.

As a young boy, Benjamin became an apprentice to his older brother, James, a printer. He remained as an apprentice to his brother until 1723, when he decided to go on his own. He arrived in Philadelphia and soon found work as an apprentice printer.

After several years as an apprentice, Franklin decided to borrow money to purchase his own printing business. This purchase would prove successful and lead to other ventures in publication including his purchase of the Pennsylvania Gazette and the publication of "Poor Richard's Almanac."

With his printing business thriving, Franklin decided on a new venture – science. Franklin invented a heat efficient stove, bifocals, and swim fins to name a few. Perhaps his most well-known contribution to science involved his famous experiment with a kite that confirmed the existence of electricity.

In Philadelphia, Franklin also was involved in civic affairs. He was involved in setting up hospitals for the sick, helping people gain access to books, and setting up a fire department. As the American Revolution approached, Franklin's citizenship would extend beyond the borders of Philadelphia.

Franklin was elected to the Second Continental Congress and helped draft the Declaration of Independence. In 1776, Franklin signed the Declaration and then traveled to France to gain their support against Great Britain in the Revolution. After America's successful defeat of the British, Franklin then signed the Constitution – the document that would establish the United States as one nation with one central government. One of his final civic acts was to write an anti-slavery treaty in 1789.

Franklin died on April 17, 1790. Some 20,000 people attended his funeral. Franklin was a great citizen of Philadelphia, America, and the world.

Benjamin Franklin Scene

Goal
- Students will be able to recognize the citizenship accomplishments of Benjamin Franklin

Description of Scene
This scene primarily focuses on Benjamin Franklin's contributions as a citizen of the United States. The scene takes place in 1776 just as Franklin is about to sign the Declaration of Independence and travel abroad to France to seek their assistance in the colonies' efforts to gain independence from the British.

Clues
- Notes on the Declaration of Independence (page 103) – to show that he was willing to sign the document accepting the risk it posed for the independence of the colonies from Great Britain
- Ship ticket to France (page 103) – to show that Franklin was willing to travel to France in support of his country – also establishes that he lived in Philadelphia
- Desk – the purpose of this clue is to hold all of the items that are primary clues
- Cover of *Poor Richard's Almanac* – this clue could help students establish the identity of Franklin
- Feather pen – this clue exists to establish the time period
- Candle – this clue exists to establish the time period

Setting Up the Scene
Reserve an approximate 10' x 8' area of your classroom. Place all clues on the desk.

Note: You may choose not to reveal Franklin's name on the cover of *Poor Richard's Almanac*.

Higher Level Activities
Discussion Questions
- Why was it important that Benjamin Franklin went to France?
- Would you have signed the Declaration of Independence? Why or why not?

Follow-up Activities
- Have students make a scrapbook of the life of Benjamin Franklin.
- In the spirit of Benjamin Franklin, have students brainstorm ways that they can be good citizens.
- Have students decide which among Franklin's accomplishments was the most important.
- Have students create another clue that may have appeared in this scene.

Investigating the Scene

1. Your big questions:

   a. To whom do these clues belong?

   b. How did this person contribute to America?

2. Mark approximate time period on the time line below.

   1700   1750   1800   1850   1900

3. List the clues you see in the scene. List important items about each clue (see page 10 ***"How to Investigate Historical Clues"*** for help).

4. What is your hypothesis about what is going on in the scene?

5. What do you need to know about each clue? List your smaller questions to help you answer the bigger questions.

6. Research your final answer to the big questions. Use the ***"Think About It"*** page to help you. Hint: The answers to your smaller questions will help you answer the bigger questions.

7. Was your hypothesis correct?

8. What else do you want to know? List other questions you have about this historical topic.

Think About It

It could be ...(choose one)

    A. Francis Scott Key

    B. Betsy Ross

    C. Benjamin Franklin

    D. Thomas Jefferson

.... because (mark the box next to the reasons **WHY**)

☐ The person lived during that time

☐ The person had written books or poems

☐ The person participated in the American Revolution

☐ The person had lived in Philadelphia

It could NOT be ...(choose one)

    A. Francis Scott Key

    B. Betsy Ross

    C. Benjamin Franklin

    D. Thomas Jefferson

..... because (mark the box next to the reasons **WHY NOT**)

☐ The person did not live during that time

☐ The person was not a writer of books or poems

☐ The person did not participate in the American Revolution

☐ The person had not lived in Philadelphia

Based upon the answers above, I think the clues belong to

_____.

Clues Provided - Benjamin Franklin

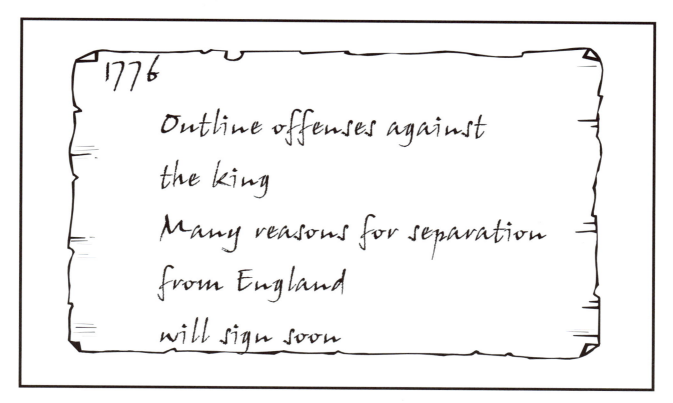

1776

Outline offenses against the king

Many reasons for separation from England

will sign soon

-------------------- Cut Here --------------------

1776
1 Person
Destination: France

Leave Philadelphia Harbor

End of Chapter Activities

1. Have students debate who contributed the most to American society among Francis Scott Key, Betsy Ross, and Benjamin Franklin.

2. Have students brainstorm ideas as to how voting may change to increase participation in the future.

3. Have students add something new to our American symbols – the Flag and the National Anthem. Students should reference how these symbols came into existence.

4. Have students assess the long-term effects that the Flag, the National Anthem, and the contributions of Benjamin Franklin had on America.